GEORGE WASHINGTON

The Father of Our Country

by BELLA KORAL

☆

Illustrated by WILLIAM HUTCHINSON

Prepared under the supervision of JOSETTE FRANK,
Children's Book Adviser of the Child Study Association of America

RANDOM HOUSE · NEW YORK

FERRY FARM

It was February 22, 1732. On that cold, raw morning, Mr. Augustine Washington stood at a window of his plantation home in Virginia watching the snow fall. He tapped his foot impatiently as he looked out toward the Potomac River.

The door opened and he turned expectantly.

"You have a son, Mr. Washington," said the smiling woman who came in. "A strapping big boy."

The baby's mother, Mary Ball Washington, wanted her first son named after the man who had been her guardian.

And so the name George Washington was given to this child who was to bring great glory to it and would come to be called "the father of his country."

When George was born, there was no country called the United States, for most of this land, stretching from the Atlantic Ocean to the Pacific, was a wilderness.

Virginia was not a state then, either, but one of thirteen colonies. Most of the people who lived in the colonies were English, or the children of English people, and the King of England ruled over them.

George's great-grandfather, John Washington, had come from England about eighty years before George was born. Like many of the early settlers of Virginia, he had built a plantation near the seacoast. Only the little strip near the sea was safe, for the rest of the land was wilderness. Tribes of Indians roamed through the forests, where they tracked down bears and wolves and fought against one another.

There were no roads such as we have today, only rough paths

through the woods. People traveled on horseback, or sailed in small boats up and down the rivers.

When George was still a little boy, the family moved to another of his father's plantations. This was on the Rappahannock River. It was called Ferry Farm.

By the time George was six, he had three younger brothers, Sam, John, and Charles, and a sister, Betty, who looked so much like him they were often taken for twins. George also had two older half-brothers, Lawrence and Austin, who were away at school.

Life was always busy on a plantation and there were many places for a boy like George to explore. He watched the carpenters, shoe-makers, and tanners working in the small shops that clustered about the main house. There were also little houses for smoking hams, for spinning wool, weaving cloth, and making candles.

Nearly all the work of the plantation, in the fields and in the little shops, was done by Negro slaves. For many years they had been brought from Africa and sold to the "planters," as the Virginia plantation owners were called.

Mr. Washington looked after the farm and shops, and his wife managed the work in the little houses.

George loved to fish and to swim in the river. He ran races and jumped fences with his brothers and dogs. He was always tall for his age, with long arms and legs. When he pitched horseshoes, his aim was sure and he could throw an iron bar farther than any boy his age. When he wrestled, George could easily down any boy his size.

He was very proud of his pony, Hero, and was a first-rate rider when he was still a small boy.

George and his brothers and sister loved to watch the barges, rowboats, sailboats, and trading ships from Boston and New York passing Ferry Farm on the broad river.

But the ship they looked forward to most was the big sailing vessel from England. It came every summer, bringing bonnets and pretty dresses for George's mother. Also it brought furniture, tools, dishes and toys—all sorts of fine things from across the sea.

When these had been unloaded at the Washingtons' place, the ship sailed on up the river leaving goods at other plantations.

On its return trip it stopped again. Now the tobacco raised on the plantation was carried aboard ship to be taken to the markets of England.

On "loading day," Negro slaves rolled the tobacco barrels, tied by ropes, down the steep bank to the river where they were caught by other slaves. As the barrels rolled down, George held his breath, for if one broke loose from the ropes, it would crash into the water and be lost. The slaves must make sure none was lost, for tobacco was used as money in Virginia and it paid for the fine things the ship brought to Ferry Farm.

George would listen to the ship's captain and think how pleasant it might be to sail away to foreign lands—perhaps to wear a fine uniform with silver buttons like the captain's!

George's first teacher was a Mr. Hobby, who taught him to spell and write. Mr. Hobby was the sexton of a church near Ferry Farm and took charge of funerals in the church graveyard besides teaching boys their letters. George learned to write beautifully with a pen, but was a poor speller all his life.

When the boy had learned all that Mr. Hobby could teach him, a Mr. Williams taught him arithmetic. George was very good at this.

Stories about George Washington as a boy have been retold so often through the years that even though we're not sure they really did happen, they have become a part of the story of America. And they do tell us something of the kind of boy he was.

One such story is about George and his father. One day Mr. Washington went for a walk in his garden. Near some gooseberry bushes he cleared a space and made it ready for planting. Then he took a stick and traced the letters of George's name in the soft earth. After that he filled the letters with seeds and patted it all down with his hands.

He chose this place near the gooseberry bushes because the berries were getting ripe—and he knew how much George loved gooseberries.

About a week later George came running into the house, his eyes shining with delight.

"Oh, Father, I must show you the most wonderful thing!" he exclaimed.

Mr. Washington let the boy lead him to the spot near the gooseberry bushes. There in large letters of soft green was the name *GEORGE WASHINGTON*.

The story most often told is the one about George and the cherry tree.

When George was about six, we're told, his father gave him a shiny new hatchet.

In the orchard were some fine fruit trees that had been sent to his father from England. George went up to a young cherry tree and drove his hatchet into its glossy trunk. The chips flew all around and in a few moments the tree fell with a crash.

When his father saw what had happened, he became very angry. He sent for George and asked, "George, do you know who cut down my cherry tree?"

The boy lowered his eyes for a long moment. Then he looked up and said, "Father, I cannot tell a lie. I did it with my little hatchet."

"George," said his father, "that was my favorite tree but I'd rather lose a thousand trees than have my son lie or be a coward."

Another story tells of George and of a sorrel colt which had been given to his mother. One day, when he was about ten, he was returning from a gallop across the fields on his pony, Hero, when he saw this colt tied to a tree in a pasture.

Two stable boys were trying to get close enough to put a bridle on him. But the colt just reared and snorted angrily.

"That's the meanest horse I ever did see," said one. "No one'll ever break him!"

"I'll ride that colt," said George quietly. He jumped off Hero and tied him to the fence.

The boys knew George was an excellent rider. They knew, too, that when he made up his mind to do something, he did it. Somehow the three of them managed to get a bridle on the wildly plunging colt. George sprang on his back and away he dashed.

Back and forth across the pasture the colt galloped, his eyes rolling wildly with fear. One moment he'd be high in the air with back arched. The next, he'd be down to earth with a thud.

But he couldn't shake off the rider.

Every moment the boys expected to see George trampled under the flying hoofs. The wild colt would not give in. And neither would George. He had made up his mind to tame this horse. No colt was

going to get the better of him.

Suddenly, more determined than ever, the colt leaped even higher into the air. But that was his last leap, for the splendid animal burst a vein and fell dead.

Sadly George went to his mother.

"Mother," he said, "I killed the sorrel colt. I didn't mean to." And then he told the whole story.

Though she was angry, Mrs. Washington did not scold him as George had expected. "What's done is done," she said. "I'm sorry the colt is dead, but I'm glad you were brave enough to tell the truth about it."

One day, when George was about ten, the English ship brought George's two half-brothers, Lawrence and Austin, home. They were the sons of George's father and his first wife.

Like the sons of other well-to-do Virginia families, Lawrence and Austin had been sent abroad to study in England. Now they were grown men, and were returning to help their father manage his plantations.

Lawrence was fourteen years older than George, and Austin was twelve years older. George was really their little brother. The two young men had been away from home so long he had to become acquainted with them all over again.

He would listen breathlessly when Lawrence told how he had fought for England in her war with Spain. George's eyes glowed as Lawrence told him about his adventures during the campaign, and especially about his brave commander, Admiral Vernon.

Lawrence became George's hero. The boy would fasten his big brother's sword about his waist and pretend he was going off to war.

George and his schoolmates played at being soldiers, carrying cornstalks for muskets and marching all over a vacant field. George was chosen captain because he knew the most about drilling. He had picked up every bit of information that came his way from his big brother. "Captain" George was strict—and no one dared talk back to the captain!

When George was eleven, his father died. His mother now had to care for her five children and to manage the plantation at Ferry Farm. Yet she found time every evening to gather her children about her and tell them stories from the Bible and to teach them to be obedient and truthful.

Great changes came to the family. According to the custom of the time, George's father had left most of his property to his eldest son, Lawrence. This was a plantation called Hunting Creek on the Potomac River, where the family had lived before coming to Ferry Farm.

Lawrence soon married Anne Fairfax, who came from a well-known Virginia family. He rebuilt the house on the Potomac that has become famous, and named it Mount Vernon after the Admiral under whom he had served.

George knew that now he could never go to school in England as his half-brothers had done. He would have to do his best with what schooling was at hand.

At the new school George now attended, the master gave him a little book called *The Rules of Civility*, containing a set of rules for good conduct and right living. Not many boys of twelve would care for such a book today, but George must have found it interesting and useful for he copied out in his fine handwriting such maxims as:

"Sleep not when others speak."
"Sit not when others stand."
"Treat others as you would yourself be treated."

There were one hundred and ten maxims, and George copied them all. Some, such as, "Cleanse not your teeth with the table cloth," seem humorous now as we look at them in George's careful handwriting.

The last maxim in the book was: "Labor to keep alive in your breast that little spark of celestial fire called conscience."

THE YOUNG SURVEYOR

When George was fourteen he began to think of his future—of earning a living. English sailing vessels on the Rappahannock had always stirred him. Why not go to sea?

He talked over his plan with Lawrence, who believed Admiral Vernon would help. It might not be long, he thought, before a bright lad like George reached a high place in the King's navy. So it was arranged.

During the following weeks George could think of nothing else. A sea captain, a friend of the family, agreed to take the boy to England with him. Young George dreamt of sailing before the mast, seeing himself as the brave young officer shouting orders to his men while bullets whizzed all around.

His clothes chest was ready to be put aboard and all his relatives came to say good-bye to him. But the ship he was to sail on brought a letter to George's mother which changed all the carefully laid plans.

"If you care for George's future," wrote the boy's uncle from England, "don't let him go to sea. He will have very little chance to become an officer. If he begins as a sailor, he'll never be anything else."

The letter convinced George's mother that his going to sea would be a sad mistake, and the ship sailed without him.

How different our country's history might have been if George had joined the English navy!

The boy was terribly disappointed, but he could not go against his mother's wishes. Since he must stay home, he decided to work and study.

One day, soon after this, he found a set of surveyor's instruments which had belonged to his father. George was delighted to discover the tripod, compass and chains used for measuring land. He had always liked arithmetic and numbers. Now he decided to study to become a surveyor.

He knew there were millions of acres of land in what was then called Virginia that had never been surveyed. The owners did not know where their land began or ended. There should be plenty of work for him to do as soon as he was ready for it.

Whenever George met a surveyor, he offered to carry the man's tripod and chains just for the chance of learning more about his work.

He was now spending many weeks at a time with Lawrence and Anne at Mount Vernon. Lawrence was like a second father to him, and George loved and admired him more than ever.

Mount Vernon became a gathering place where important visitors came and went, among them many English officers. There were gay parties and balls in the evening and fox-hunts in the morning. It was here that young George acquired the courtesy and dignity that distinguished him all the rest of his life.

Still he kept on practicing his surveying. Scarcely a day passed that he was not out on the plantation measuring his brother's fields.

His work was so neat and accurate that soon he began to earn money helping other surveyors. On his trips he saw many fine parcels of land, and he began to save his earnings to buy land for himself.

By the time George was sixteen, he was over six feet tall and stood as straight as an Indian. He could ride as if he'd been born on a horse and was a good wrestler and first-rate shot, too.

We're told that once he picked up a piece of slate the size of a silver dollar and threw it across the Rappahannock at Fredericksburg. The slate fell at least thirty feet on the other side of the river. Many other strong men have tried it since, but not one has ever been able to match this feat.

It was at Mount Vernon that George met Lord Thomas Fairfax, an elderly Englishman who had come to live in America. Lord Fairfax, a soldier who had seen a great deal of the world, owned great tracts of land that had never been surveyed. He liked the way George rode a horse, and they often went fox-hunting together. Soon they became fast friends.

Lord Fairfax gave George books to read, and from their talks together the boy learned about England's history and its laws as well as its wars.

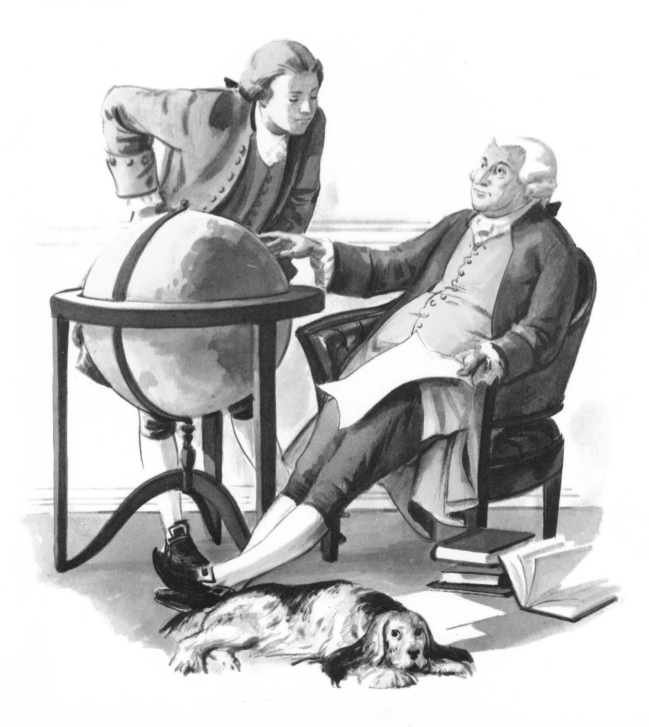

The elderly Englishman saw how brave young George was and how careful and exact in everything he did. He noticed that George measured his brother's turnip fields as if he were planning a town. So, before long, he asked George to be one of the party of surveyors he was sending out to measure his property. He hoped that after the land was surveyed and divided into farms, more settlers would go there to live.

On a bright March day, George and his companions rode out onto

the wilderness trails. The forests were so dense that the surveyors could travel only a small distance each day. Sometimes they had to swim their horses across the streams. Now and then they came upon little clearings where backwoodsmen and their families lived.

At night, wrapped in a blanket, George slept before a campfire, or in a hut. Once, when his straw bed caught fire, he was nearly burned to death.

One day a band of thirty Indian braves wearing war paint and feathers slipped into the camp. They were the first wild Indians George had ever seen. Some had scalps dangling from their belts, for they were returning home from war with another tribe. However, they were friendly to the surveyors, who gave them gifts and asked them to perform their war dance.

When evening came, the warriors cleared a large circle and began gathering wood. Soon a roaring fire was blazing in the clearing.

One of the Indians borrowed a pot, filled it half full of water, and stretched a deerskin over it. That was the drum. Another brave made music by filling a gourd with gunshot that rattled when he shook it.

The fire burned brightly, lighting up the bronzed bodies of the Indians. Their knives and tomahawks gleamed as they danced around the flames, singing and shouting their war cries.

George thought the dance was very comical. Later that night by candlelight he wrote about it in his copybook. This would be something to tell his friends about when he got home.

Lord Fairfax was so pleased with George's report of the surveying trip that he arranged to have his young friend chosen surveyor for the county. With the money he earned, George bought more land.

For the next three years the young county surveyor spent much time at his work in the Virginia wilderness. There he learned the ways of backwoodsmen and Indians, and how to face danger with courage. He learned to be prepared for anything; and he learned how to lead men.

Between surveying trips, George learned from Lawrence and Lord Fairfax enough about military tactics to become a major in the Virginia militia.

A LEADER OF TROOPS

But now there came a sad time for George. His brother Lawrence became very ill. George went with him to the West Indies, hoping the warm climate would help him. It was the only time George was ever to leave his native land. But the warm climate did not help Lawrence.

On a hot July day, soon after his return, Lawrence died. When his estate was settled, George became the master of Mount Vernon. But he was not to be allowed to remain there peacefully just yet.

For some time trouble had been brewing in the colonies.

Frenchmen were coming down from Canada and claiming land that the English said belonged to their King. They were building forts and, with the help of Indians friendly to them, were driving out Virginia backwoodsmen who had gone into the wilderness to build settlements.

The Governor of Virginia wanted to put an end to this. He decided to send a message to the French Commander ordering him to stop building the forts and to let the Virginia backwoodsmen live peacefully in their settlements.

For such a mission, the Governor needed a brave, skillful, determined man who knew the wilderness well. And so he chose young Major George Washington.

With a few Indians, some hunters, and a guide named Gist, Washington started on the dangerous journey.

Deep in the wilderness was the village of a famous Indian chief named Half King who had been quarreling with the French. Washington's party set out to find this village and win the help of Half King. The chieftain became friendly with Washington, and with his help the men reached the French fort safely.

To the Virginia Governor's message, the French Commander replied that he had been ordered to hold that fort and would stay just where he was!

It was December by the time Washington and Gist started back. Most of the time they had to go on foot, for horses could not travel through the trackless woods at that time of year. The ground was covered with snow and in some places the rivers were frozen.

At one place they met an Indian who insisted on being their guide. When they were deep in the woods, he suddenly turned and fired his musket at them! Luckily he missed. The two men caught him and Gist would have shot him then and there. But George would not permit this. So they sent the treacherous false guide away. Then they traveled all night, for they were afraid the Indian would return, looking for their scalps!

Washington and Gist planned to cross the Allegheny River by walking over the ice. But now they found it was only partly frozen. Great cakes of ice were floating through the open waters.

They began to cut down trees to build a raft. Since they had only one hatchet between them, it took them all day. While they were trying to steer their raft between the cakes of ice, George was pitched into the water. Almost drowned, he struggled back on board, his clothing frozen stiff.

The two freezing men spent that bitterly cold night on an island. When morning came, the ice on the river was firm and they were able to walk to the opposite side. There they found shelter and warmth at a trading post.

After many such adventures, Washington came safely back with the French Commander's reply to the Governor, and his own report of what he had found out.

Everywhere people in the colony praised young Washington's skill as the leader of the expedition. They saw that here was a man whose wisdom and courage they could trust. And soon the Governor appointed Washington a lieutenant-colonel of Virginia troops.

In the meantime the King of England had learned how the French were building forts along the Ohio and how their traders were coming closer to the Virginia colony.

"If we allow this to go on, they will soon take all our western country from us," he said.

The very next winter he sent over an army under General Braddock to drive the French from that part of America and to teach their Indian friends a lesson.

General Braddock had heard of the fearless young Washington who knew the western wilderness so well, so he invited him to be his aide. George was happy to accept the post. He could learn a great deal, he thought, from a general who was famous for his fighting on the battlefields of Europe.

What a handsome sight Braddock's army made as the red-coated troops stepped from the boats! They marched in perfect order, and every button on every uniform sparkled.

Washington's colonial soldiers did not wear uniforms, as the English soldiers did. Instead, like the Indians, they wore buckskin shirts and fringed leggings. The English sometimes made fun of them, calling them "Buckskins."

Braddock's army was to attack a French fort near where Pittsburgh now stands. The English General and his men had never fought in the wilderness, nor did they know how an Indian steals up behind his enemy.

"Indians do not fight like your armies," Washington warned Braddock. "They don't fight in battle formation, but behind trees and rocks where no one can see them."

"Our troops know how to return bullets," Braddock replied proudly. "It would be too bad if British troops could not meet a handful of naked Indians."

The fine army in brilliant scarlet coats marched in proud array through a narrow road in the forest. They were not far now from the French fort they were planning to attack.

Suddenly shots rang out from behind the rocks and trees, and the woods echoed with Indian war yells.

The English troops were so dazed at this new kind of fighting where they could not see the enemy, that they ran like sheep. In trying to escape, they blocked the way of their own men, who were shot down like animals in a pen.

The "Buckskins," of course, knew how to meet the Indians. They took cover behind trees, too, and returned the fire of the redskins.

The war cries of the Indians filled the air with a dreadful noise. From time to time a half-naked brave would dart from behind a tree, brandishing his tomahawk. Then he would take a scalp and disappear again.

Through all the confusion Washington rode into the thickest of the danger. It was he who helped save the English from being entirely wiped out.

Bullets whizzed by his head—one ripped through his hat, and three more sliced through his uniform as Washington carried Braddock's orders to his men. But he was not hurt. Two horses were shot from under him and he jumped onto the back of a third. It was a miracle that he escaped.

Braddock was not so lucky. It was not until he was wounded that he gave orders to retreat. Washington helped carry him from the battlefield in a litter made of his scarlet sash.

Four days later Braddock died, grateful that his aide, Washington, was at his side. He was buried there in the road, where the army wagons rolled over the spot to hide his grave from Indian scalp-hunters.

Afterward, an old Indian chief said he had told all his braves to aim at Washington, but that they could not hit him. "He will never die in battle," said the warrior, "but will become a chief of nations."

When the people heard the news of Braddock's terrible defeat, they were grieved. But they were proud of Washington, who had saved the remnant of the English Army and had upheld the honor of the "Buckskins." He was named Commander-in-Chief of the Virginia troops and became renowned throughout the colonies.

For three years after Braddock's defeat, Washington commanded troops in the west. Finally the French were driven back to Canada by fresh armies from England and by colonial troops in the north.

COMMANDER-IN-CHIEF

Now Washington began to think of finding a wife, for he was twenty-six years old. When he met Mrs. Martha Custis, a pretty widow with two small children, he knew he had found his life's partner. Martha owned a plantation near Williamsburg, then the capital of Virginia. She was plump and small; Washington was tall and slim. She was lively and gay; he was serious and dignified.

One day Washington wrote his English merchants to send him, for his wedding, "enough velvet to make a coat, waistcoat and breeches for a tall man, with a silk button to suit it."

George and Martha had a fashionable wedding to which the best-known people of Virginia were invited.

After the ceremony the bride was driven home in a coach drawn by six white horses, while Washington rode alongside on a magnificent chestnut-brown horse.

It was the beginning of a new life for George Washington.

George and Martha were happy at Mount Vernon. A stream of guests enjoyed the dinners, dances, and fox-hunts at the plantation, for Martha was a fine hostess.

George's nickname for her was "Patsy," and when they were alone she called him her "old man."

Whenever she wanted to ask a special favor of him, she would hold onto his coat button and look up at him and smile. Washington himself seldom smiled, though when anything really amused him, he laughed so heartily that tears came to his eyes.

He came to love Martha's little boy and girl as if they were his own, and they loved him dearly, too. Washington gave them ponies to ride and bought baby dolls for the little girl.

At the time of his marriage, Washington was elected a member of the Virginia House of Burgesses. He represented the people of his county and helped to make some of the laws of the colony.

The fifteen years that followed were peaceful, happy years. Washington lived the life of a gentleman farmer. Every morning at sunrise he was on his horse riding around his fields.

He loved farming and he planned the sowing and harvesting of his crops. He tried to discover the best way to make things grow and experimented with seeds and soil.

Martha attended to the bakeshop, the spinning, the weaving, and the preserving. Her husband raised cattle, race horses, and hunting dogs. He knew what to do if an animal was in trouble and could set a dog's broken leg or cure it of the mange.

At night while Martha sat near him knitting, George figured his accounts and wrote in his diary.

Washington would have liked nothing better than to spend the rest of his life in this home he loved.

But storm clouds were gathering.

Until now, the colonists had always thought of England as their old home, their mother country. They were loyal to the King and when the new King, George III, came to the throne soon after the French and Indian War ended, the colonists drank toasts to his health. "Long live George the Third!" they cried.

The King appointed governors for most of the colonies, but each colony had an assembly chosen by the people to make its own laws.

The French and Indian War had cost England huge sums of money. So the new King, George III, decided to get more money from the colonies to pay for it.

George III was stubborn and unwise. Soon new unfair laws were being sent out from England for the colonies to obey.

The King made laws forcing the colonists to trade only with England. They were to send their tobacco, corn and cotton to pay for all the goods they bought.

Then the King put an extra price or tax on almost everything the colonists bought. Orders came that the colonists must not even drink a cup of tea without paying England a tax on it.

One dark night fifty men in Boston, dressed like Indians to disguise themselves, climbed on board an English ship loaded with tea. Quietly and swiftly they dumped every box of tea overboard. Rather than pay a tax on tea, these people would drink no tea at all.

To punish Boston for this "tea party," the King ordered the harbor closed. No ships could come in or go out. This meant hunger and suffering for the people of Boston. Besides this, the King sent his troops to arrest or shoot anyone who would not obey his commands.

At this all the colonies were bitter and angry. Washington stood up in the Virginia assembly and said, "I'm willing to raise a thousand men at my own expense to march to the relief of Boston."

But the people of Virginia were not yet ready to go so far.

All the colonies wrote to one another, and finally it was decided they would all act together. A congress was called at Philadelphia to which all of them sent delegates. Washington was chosen from Virginia.

"Let us still hope for peace and justice," he told the congress.

The people were anxious. Would the King ever give back their rights to the colonies? The congress sent him a petition begging him not to enforce his unjust laws.

No answer came to that petition. The colonists saw with sorrow that they might have to fight for their rights, so they began to drill and arm their own soldiers.

In the House of Burgesses at Williamsburg, a young man, Patrick Henry, made a speech saying the King had no right to tax the people without their consent. "Taxation without representation is tyranny!" he said. He also said, "Give me liberty or give me death!" Washington heard this speech and believed Patrick Henry was right.

Washington was asked to train the men of his county, and he agreed. Though he loved peace, he said, "No man should hesitate to use arms in defense of freedom."

Then in the spring of 1775 came the dreaded news. The King's redcoats had been growing more haughty and insulting every day.

One day in April, a company of redcoats started secretly toward Concord, not far from Boston, to seize arms and gunpowder the colonists had stored there. News of their plans was spread by swift riders in the night. Quickly farmers and townspeople seized their muskets and gathered quietly at Lexington to stop the British. Shots were fired by both sides and many men were killed.

And here, with this Battle of Lexington, began the long Revolutionary War.

Again a congress was called together in Philadelphia. Washington appeared in his blue-and-buff uniform of a Virginia colonel. It was his way of saying to the congress, "The time for fighting has come and I am ready."

The delegates voted to make this congress the government of the thirteen colonies, and they made Washington Commander-in-Chief of their armies. No other man in America knew as much about war as he, and no other was so well fitted to command. He refused to accept any money for his services.

He was already on his way to take command of the army around Boston when a breathless messenger arrived, bringing news of the greatest importance. "There's been a big battle at Bunker Hill," he told Washington. "We lost the hill, but our men held it against three attacks by the British before they retreated."

"Then our country's liberties are safe," said Washington.

Seated on his splendid white charger under a giant elm, Washington took command of his army at Cambridge. It was an odd army — the men dressed as they happened to come from shop or farm. And they were poorly armed and half-trained.

How could they stand up against the well-trained and well-armed redcoats? Yet those shabbily dressed men were brave. They loved their country and would defend it with all their might! It was the first *American* army.

Washington took off his hat and, drawing his shining sword, raised
it high before the cheering crowd while the cannon thundered.

In a few months General Washington trained these men so well that the redcoats, knowing they could not hold out, sailed away from Boston. At last the city was free.

But the General knew they would attack New York, so he moved his army to that city. And there wonderful news came from Philadelphia. On the Fourth of July, 1776, the colonies had declared themselves free from England! King George would never again rule over them!

When Washington received a copy of the Declaration, he had it read aloud to his men. Happy to know they were no longer subjects

of the English King, they rushed to the park where stood a statue of George III on horseback. They pulled it down, knocked off its head, and melted the rest to make bullets.

The Declaration of Independence made the colonies a free and independent nation. Now the men of the new army had something even more precious to fight for. It was their own country, and they would keep it free.

Washington had few men compared to the English, and fewer guns. His men seldom had enough to eat, and they were fighting against a well-armed, well-trained, well-fed army.

Washington often had to retreat, but he had a surprising trick of turning and attacking the redcoats just as they thought they had beaten him. He held on patiently through long discouraging years. He had firm faith in his cause even when many others thought all was lost.

As time went by Washington's army grew smaller. His men were hungry, tired, and cold and would leave camp when their enlisted time was up. Congress had little money or supplies to send them.

VALLEY FORGE

Yet, after many narrow escapes, this "ragged Continental" army managed to reach Pennsylvania across the Delaware River. It was December and the river was half-frozen. Washington knew the British were waiting for the river to freeze solid. Then they could march over it and destroy the American army.

But Washington had a daring plan. On the New Jersey side of the river, in the town of Trenton, the British and their hired troops, the Hessians, were preparing to celebrate Christmas. Washington decided to surprise them!

In the wind and sleet of that stormy night, Washington's men rowed across the river, pushing their boats through great cakes of floating ice. Some of them were barefoot and they shivered in their rags. The path they took to the river was marked by their bloody footprints in

the snow. But somehow they managed to get themselves and their horses and cannon across the icy Delaware.

The Hessian troops, full of food and wine after their Christmas dinner, were sleeping soundly. At dawn they were awakened by the sound of American guns—and could hardly believe what was happening. After a short battle the dazed Hessians and their British officers had to surrender.

Washington's men gained new courage, and his victory at Trenton was a Christmas gift that brought great joy to the new nation.

But there were more hardships in store for the Americans.

The next winter, while the British were comfortable in Philadelphia, which they had captured, Washington's army camped at nearby Valley Forge.

Deep snow lay on the ground, and the men had to build log huts for shelter. They had no shoes and wrapped their feet in rags. The bitter wind blew through their tattered clothes as they dragged logs from the forest. At night they hadn't enough blankets to keep them warm. Until their huts were finished, they built great brush fires and lay with their feet toward the flames.

And there was very little to eat. Many became ill and died of hunger and disease. Some left camp because they could no longer endure the suffering.

Washington stayed in a tent close to his men, sharing their hardships, until their huts were finished. Then he made his headquarters in a small stone house.

Martha Washington came to spend the winter close to her soldier-husband. With a basket of food on her arm, she went from hut to hut to comfort the soldiers who were ill.

Washington's heart was heavy with suffering for his men and he kept begging Congress to send him money and supplies. Still he kept up his courage, standing firm and holding on even when it seemed as if the terrible winter would never end.

But before that winter was over, a young soldier, the Marquis de Lafayette, whose family held a high position in France, arrived at Valley Forge. He had heard of Washington and of America's struggle for freedom, and had made up his mind to help.

A warm friendship sprang up between Washington and young Lafayette, who soon became the General's aide. This young man contributed nobly to the American cause.

When spring came, food carts and supply wagons began to roll into camp. The men were cheered and Washington's hopes rose.

Then one day came glorious news. France was joining America in the war! America was no longer fighting alone against England. French ships would soon be coming.

Washington heard the news with quiet joy. Lafayette threw his arms about the General and, in the French fashion, kissed him on both cheeks.

THE BRITISH SURRENDER

But even with French help, three more years of struggle dragged on. Hard, bloody battles were fought in the North and South but Washington's faith never failed.

In October, 1781, a large British Army led by General Cornwallis was trapped at Yorktown, Virginia. American guns had fired at the British forts for ten days, and French ships had bottled up the redcoats from the sea. The British finally had to give up and they sent out a man with a white flag of truce.

With his officers Washington rode to the meadow where the redcoats were to surrender. He sat on his horse and watched the scene from a slight distance.

The British marched down the field between rows of French and American soldiers. Drums rolled as man after man laid down his musket. Then the British General handed his sword to an American officer.

A great victory had been won! Washington had worked hard and waited long years for this moment. "The work is done, and well done," he said quietly to a friend standing near by.

However, for Washington the war was not over yet. So long as a single British soldier remained on American soil, Washington would still have work to do.

Two years later, King George III had to admit that his thirteen colonies were now the United States of America, and a peace treaty was signed. Our country was truly free and independent!

When the last British soldier had sailed from New York, Washington felt his task was done. There, at Fraunces Tavern, in a room you may see today, he came to say farewell to his officers. His heart was full, for he remembered the defeats and hardships they had suffered. Now he told them they must preserve with all their strength the nation they had fought so hard to build.

As the officers passed by, Washington embraced each one affectionately as he said good-bye.

OUR FIRST PRESIDENT

At last, after eight years of war, Washington came back on Christmas Eve to his beloved Mount Vernon. Shouts of welcome from the delighted servants greeted their master.

At the door were Martha and her grandchildren, Nelly and George Washington Custis, to welcome him. Nelly was four and little George was two. They were the children of Martha's son, Jacky, who had died after the battle of Yorktown. Washington and his wife had adopted them as their own children. He gathered them into his arms.

Now Washington planned to pass the rest of his life peacefully at Mount Vernon. There was a great deal to do, for he wanted his home to be as beautiful as he could make it. He had lawns and driveways laid out and planted many trees and shrubs. He was happy to be just a busy farmer once again, making the rounds of his plantation on horseback.

Mount Vernon was always filled with company. Important people from all over the world kept coming to pay their respects to George Washington. Painters and sculptors arrived to make portraits of the greatest man in the country.

Washington could not turn visitors away. But sometimes he preferred to be with Nelly and little George. They loved to visit Nelson, his old war horse, and Washington would take them to the pasture to pat Nelson's forehead when the horse trotted over to greet his master.

Gifts from abroad kept arriving by boat at Mount Vernon—trees and plants for the gardens, and animals for the farms. The King of Spain sent a valuable long-eared jackass, called Royal Gift. A servant proudly led the animal around the countryside, calling, "Make way for the jackass of the King of Spain!" Everyone came out to stare at Royal Gift because he belonged to Washington.

During this time Washington received thousands of letters from people interested in the affairs of the country.

He was becoming more and more troubled, for these letters told him things were not going well with the thirteen states. They had begun to quarrel with one another as soon as the war ended. They were not really *united*.

Wise men saw that something must be done to save the country. So a great convention was held in Philadelphia to make a set of rules—a Constitution—to govern the *whole* country.

The convention chose George Washington to preside over it. There were many stormy arguments by the delegates, but his calm wisdom was always there to guide them.

That convention brought forth a great and wonderful work. It framed

the rules, or Constitution, by which our country has been governed ever since.

According to the Constitution, the people were to elect a president for the new government. They chose a man they loved and honored above all others—George Washington. They knew he would be faithful to the new republic, that he was wise and just and that the welfare of the nation could be entrusted to him.

Washington had hoped he might spend the rest of his years as a farmer at Mount Vernon. But when the people called him to serve, he could not shirk his duty. He could only pray for strength and wisdom for the great task ahead.

So in April, 1789, Washington again left his beloved Mount Vernon. He set out for New York, which was the first capital of our country.

All along the way parades and celebrations were held in his honor. Outside Philadelphia he was met by a company of soldiers. With flags waving and drums rolling, they escorted him in his blue-and-buff uniform through throngs of cheering people.

Near Trenton, where he had crossed the Delaware in 1776, a great arch had been erected. There Washington was presented with a magnificent white horse. As he rode under the arch, young girls dressed in white scattered flowers before him and sang a song of welcome.

He crossed the Hudson in a splendid barge decked with flags and rowed by thirteen oarsmen in white uniforms.

As Washington reached the city of New York, all the bells rang out. Crowds shouted and cheered his name and cannons roared. Houses were bright with flags and bunting and every window and roof-top was filled with his admirers. Never had New York looked so gay.

As the final ceremony took place, Washington stood on the balcony of Federal Hall looking down into the faces of the people. He wore a brown coat and knee breeches of material made in America. The silver buttons on his coat were stamped with the American eagle and he wore his dress sword at his side.

The wild cheers were hushed as Washington stepped forward and

laid his hand on a big Bible. Slowly, and with a voice that rang out clearly, he repeated the oath that every President has taken since that day.

"I do solemnly swear that I will faithfully execute the office of President of the United States and will to the best of my ability preserve, protect, and defend the Constitution of the United States."

"God bless George Washington! Long live our President!" cried the cheering people. They loved and trusted him, for he was wise, fearless and strong.

To them he was, indeed, and would always be for all Americans, "first in war, first in peace, and first in the hearts of his countrymen."

GEORGE
WASHINGTON